it's your
move

YOUR GUIDE TO MOVING
TO SECONDARY SCHOOL

D0538210

This book was given to Ellie

By Gwenth

Date:

In preparation for moving to secondary school!

© Scripture Union 2012
It's Your Move! first published 2000, this all-new edition published 2012
ISBN 978 1 84427 6875

Scripture Union England and Wales
207–209 Queensway, Bletchley, Milton Keynes, MK2 2EB
www.scriptureunion.org.uk
Scripture Union Scotland: www.suscotland.org.uk
Scripture Union Northern Ireland: www.suni.co.uk
Scripture Union Republic of Ireland: www.scriptureunion.ie

All rights reserved. No part of this publication may be reproduced, stored in
a retrieval system, or transmitted in any form or by any means, electronic,
mechanical, photocopying, recording or otherwise, without the prior
permission of Scripture Union.

The right of Robert Harrison to be identified as the author of the stories on
pages 31-35 and 41-45 has been asserted by him in accordance with the
Copyright, Designs and Patents Act 1988.

Scripture quotations are from the Contemporary English Version published
by HarperCollinsPublishers © 1991, 1992, 1995 American Bible Society.

British Library Cataloguing-in-Publication Data
A catalogue record of this book is available from the British Library.

Printed and bound in India by Nutech Print Services
Cover and internal design: Martin Lore

With special thanks to: Nick Harding, Amy Stock from schoolswork.co.uk,
Rachel Foster from Bridgebuilder Trust, Andrew Phillips from Christians in
Schools Trust, Dave Mockett from COOL (in association with SU Scotland),
Wayne Dixon and other Scripture Union schools development workers, Anna
Williams, Alicia Wallace, Ian Butt and pupils and teachers from St Ethelbert's,
St Bernard's, St Bernadette's, Rickley Park and Plockton High

ALL ABOUT ME!

Name Ellie

Date of birth 22nd Jan

Primary school Carleton

Me!!

Best friends Rianna

Favourite subject ART

Favourite teachers Mrs Gini

Secondary school Auchmuty

Favourite food Tuna Pasta bake

Three favourite things to do

Welcome to It's
Your Move! – this is
your book!

Drama KS3	Date: / /

Your Target Level:

Current → Target

To reach your target you must:

GET READY FOR A NEW START!

So, you're almost at the end of primary school! SATs are over and you might be involved in an end-of-year show or a leavers' assembly. You might be able to do some of the following things in the few weeks left before the summer holidays to get ready for what's next.

MEET SECONDARY SCHOOL TEACHERS

You may have been visited by some teachers from your new secondary school. They'll tell you lots of useful stuff about what the school's like: the building, how it's going to be different, timetables and teachers. You may even have met some of the young people who are currently in Year 7.

TRANSITION DAYS/ INDUCTION DAYS/ TRANSFER DAYS

Whatever you call the day when you visit your new secondary school, make the most of it! Make the best impression you can. You're getting a new start, so if you want to make a positive change about yourself, this is your chance to do it. If you get to go there more than once, so much the better – it's a great opportunity to lose your fears and meet new people.

DIDN'T GET YOUR FIRST CHOICE?

If your new school isn't your first choice, you still have the chance to make the best of it! Each school has good things going for it so look for the positives. Don't worry about the school you wanted to go to. Enjoy where you are going.

If you're worried about anything, you can ask your Year 6 teacher now – don't spend the whole summer worrying about it.

Collect the signatures of the people you want to remember from your current school (and their phone numbers, if that's OK with them!).

AUTOGRAPHS

/ Ellie Cunliffe ♡

I keep in touch with my friends by carrier pigeon!

40

SURVIVAL TOP 40!

YOUR COUNTDOWN TO A GREAT START AT SECONDARY SCHOOL!

40

ARGUMENTS

Moving school is a stressful time, so don't be too hard on yourself if you feel like you're getting wound up. You might end up arguing with your parents or old school friends about the daftest things. Just count to ten or walk away, and if you've already said something you shouldn't have, you might need to apologise…

39

QUIET PEOPLE

We're all different! And you're going to meet a lot more different people at your new school. Some will be loud, some quiet. Some will talk all the time, some won't. There's nothing wrong with either. If you're more of an extrovert, be yourself but be sensitive to others. Quiet people make good friends because they actually listen to you!

38

KIT

You'll have lots of stuff that you'll need to remember to take to school, and it'll be different each day. There may be some kind of penalty for forgetting, so make sure you get into a routine fairly quickly. This will help you remember your essential kit for each day – anything from sports clothes to calculators!

37

EXERCISE

You'll get the chance to try out lots of different sports at your new school, so if you didn't like PE at your old school, you might find something you like here. Getting changed for PE can be a bit embarrassing – see *36 Size* – but exercise can help you develop your physique and feel good about yourself. We can't all be gold medallists, but always try to do your best – and enjoy yourself!

36

SIZE

Look around at your new year group and you'll see some people who are almost fully grown and others who are still really small! Everyone develops at a different rate. If you're smaller or less physically developed, don't worry – you'll soon have your growth spurt.

I'm the best at playing Tiddlywinks!

35

ZITS

Adolescence (when you and your body are changing) can bring zits, spots, acne, or whatever you want to call them. Try not to pick spots as this may spread the infection from one place to another. If you suffer really badly, your doctor should be able to offer some help.

34

DRUGS

Just say no. That's the best advice you can get. Illegal drugs are bad news and can get you into serious trouble, not only with the school and the police, but also with your health. It may be tempting to experiment, but drugs can cause long-term damage. If you come across them at school, walk away and report it – you'll be helping others as well as yourself.

NO DRUG

33

PSHE/
CITIZENSHIP/PSD

This subject has lots of different names, depending on your school and where you live, and it covers a wide range of topics looking at how you develop as a person. It includes health, relationships and sex, developing confidence, and making the most of your abilities. It should also help you become an informed and active citizen in society.

32

BOYS (FOR GIRLS)

You'll have plenty of new boys to get to know (unless you're at a girls-only school!) and you might think this is good! Or bad! Some will seem a bit immature, but others will be worth getting to know as friends. And you don't need to get a boyfriend too quickly – having lots of friends is much more fun!

31

GIRLS (FOR BOYS)

You're going to meet lots of girls in your new school (unless you're at a boys-only school!), and you might think this is brilliant! (Or you might not!) Try to get to know girls as your friends and keep the friendships you had with the girls in your old school. Don't worry about getting a girlfriend yet – there's enough new stuff to get used to without that too!

30

MONEY

You probably feel like you always need more money than you have! But money isn't always available, so decide what you really need money for (maybe the bus or lunch). Don't carry too much cash though, as it may get lost or taken.

29

RELIGIOUS STUDIES (RS/RE/RME)

Faith, religion and spirituality are vital to many people. It's important to understand different faiths (and what it means to have no faith), and how they influence attitudes and behaviour. RS will help you explore these different religions. Christians believe in God and follow his ways, as shown in the Bible. They believe that Jesus came to show us what God is like and how God wants us to live our lives.

28

ASSEMBLIES

In your new school, assemblies may seem shorter (and perhaps less fun!). Some will include prayers or times of quiet. Use those opportunities to think about what is said. You might want to think quietly, or pray for yourself and others.

27

CLUBS

There will be plenty of clubs at your new school – chances to play more sport, learn a musical instrument or develop other interests! Some schools have a Christian Union, which is a club where young people can go to find out more about God. Check out pages 58-9 to see what clubs you might like to join.

26

BOOKS (AND E-BOOKS!)

At school, there will be plenty of books! Text books, fiction books, reference books… Try to read what you need for each lesson (either in a paper book or an e-book) and search out books which will help you at school and in your life. The school library is an excellent place to start!

If you like reading, why not check out the studies on pages 31 and 41!

HELLO

25

OFFICE

Most school office staff are very friendly and helpful! Once you're settled in, you'll be able to work out a bit more clearly how the school office can help you. Don't be scared to ask!

24

MOBILES

Many schools don't let you bring in your phone, so leave it at home! Even if your school allows it, you might want to go without it anyway, as it's easy to lose something so small in such a big place!

23

LOOS

School toilets are sometimes not the cleanest or most pleasant places in the world. Find out where they are on your induction day, so that when you need to go, you know where to go!

22

LONELINESS

You might be worried that you'll be lonely at school, but you'll soon make new friends as you mix in with others. Everyone feels lonely at different times. If it gets too much, talk to your form tutor about it. Many people also find that a faith in God really helps. Why not have a look at the Bible poem on page 26?

21

SOCIAL NETWORKS

Facebook and other social networking websites are all over the place and you may know people who use them. However, remember that the lower age limit for Facebook and many others is 13, so you won't be old enough to register for a while yet. Be careful when you're online, as people may not actually be who they seem to be. If you're doubtful about someone, block them. Remember, if you're being bullied online (or via a mobile), tell someone about it (see 12 – Bullying).

20

PARENTS AND CARERS

Despite being old and out of touch, parents and carers want to know how their kids are getting on. They want you to be happy and to be the best you can be, and they will worry! Tell them about the good and difficult bits of school – they don't just want to nag all the time; they really do care and want to help! For a parent's point of view, check out page 62.

19

DETENTION

Some schools may keep students in at break, lunchtime or after school if they break school rules or forget homework. Try to keep out of detention, as it only wastes your time (and the teacher's time too!). If you end up in detention, behave yourself while you're there, otherwise you'll end up in another one!

18

YOUNGEST

Being the youngest (and possibly the smallest) in your school could make you feel a bit scared. But you'll soon settle in and before long you'll feel like a confident old-timer! Want proof? Check out the stories from Year 7s on pages 54–57.

17

HEADS

There are lots of different 'heads' in school – heads of year, deputy or assistant heads, heads of subjects, not forgetting the head teacher! The senior management team (the teachers in charge of running the school) all have special roles and are there to make sure you learn and do well. Don't be scared of them!

16

BREAK

It might take you a few weeks to get used to breaktime in your new school. It may help to stay with people in your tutor group for a while until you feel a bit more confident to move and mix a bit.

I Love FOOD !!! (except for some veg)

15

CANTEEN

Being at secondary school might mean that you have a better choice of food! The canteen can get noisy and confusing, but follow what others do. Make sure you buy a proper lunch rather than spending all your money on sweets, otherwise you'll be hungry all afternoon. And try not to drop your tray on the first day!

I wonder if they'll have my favourite – chocolate and pickle flavour crisps!

Rules aren't just there to annoy you – they keep you safe!

14

WEBSITE

Your new school's website is a good source of information before you start, both for you and your parents or carers. When you start your new school, it will be essential to keep checking the site as lots of information will appear there! Your teachers will tell you when you need to visit it too.

13

RULES

All schools have rules, and they are there to keep you (and everyone else) safe. Find out what the rules are and stick to them. If you don't, you'll find you're stuck with detentions (see *19 – Detention*), report cards and letters sent to your parents or carers. Not a great start!

12

BULLYING

There's no excuse for bullying. If you think you're being bullied – or someone you know – (and that includes cyberbullying online or via your phone), don't let it go on. Tell someone: a teacher, a parent or an adult you can trust. Bullies often have bad stuff going on in their lives, and telling someone will help them as well as you. Page 23 gives a bit more advice!

11

JOURNEY

Your journey to your new school might be much longer than before and you might need to use public transport. Give yourself extra time to get there in your first week, so that you have a bit of space in case anything goes wrong. If you're late, give an honest reason why – teachers have heard all the rubbish excuses before! You'll soon meet people who go the same way as you, so you won't feel lonely on the bus or walking to school.

10

TESTS AND EXAMS

Tests and exams have been part of your school life so far, and (unfortunately, you might think!) they'll carry on being important. They'll help you decide what you're good at and what you might want to do in the future. Prepare well for tests, do your best and don't panic!

I HATE EXAMS

9

UNIFORM

Your new school uniform might be formal and involve ties, shirts and blazers! Uniforms are there to help the students feel united and look at least a bit smart! Check out the rules on what you can or cannot wear before you start and you'll look your best and ready to go!

Have a go at designing your own uniform on page 46!

00291

LATE BUS TICKET

This ticket entitles the holder to one journey on the late bus and must be presented to the driver when boarding. School Code of Conduct on Buses & Coaches applies

8

Miss

HOMEWORK

There's no escape! Get into the habit of setting aside a regular time each day to do it – use your homework timetable to plan. Try not to get behind, as it can be difficult to catch up. However, if things do start to get on top of you, tell your teachers. Check out page 63 for some top tips.

7

TEACHERS

You're likely to have many more teachers than you have at primary school, with different teachers for different subjects. Some teachers seem friendly, others less so, but don't let that put you off. They're there to help you learn, so ask questions or tell them if you don't understand.

6

FORM/ GUIDANCE TEACHER

This is the teacher who checks the register for your form group and deals with any problems. They are chosen carefully because they are approachable and helpful. Don't be afraid to tell them if things aren't going right, especially at the start of school. They're there to help you!

5

FINDING YOUR WAY

Any new place can be confusing, and your new school is no exception! If you can, use a map. By the end of the first week, you'll have a good idea of where you should be going. And remember, it's better to ask than to go the wrong way and end up barging into a Year-10 Spanish lesson!

> Remember – teachers are normal people and have problems and moods like everyone else! See page 60 for proof!

4

TIMETABLE

This will be your key to knowing what you're meant to do and where you should be! Study it carefully and make sure you ask any questions at the start of term so you're happy that you know what you're supposed to do.

3 FRIENDS

You may feel a bit lost and lonely if your friends from primary school are not going to be with you – but you won't be the only one! And it may be that one or two old friends decide they want to make new friends instead. Don't worry about that. Very soon you'll find someone who's got things in common with you and a new friendship will begin. Make an effort to talk to those who seem to be on their own and you'll find yourself making new friends that way too!

2 CHOICES

You will have to make lots of choices about loads of different things, including friends, clubs, sports, or even what to eat for lunch! And, of course, there are all the different choices we make about how to act and behave in lots of different situations. To make all these choices, you'll need some help and advice, so talk to teachers, parents and friends. Many people ask God to help them make the right decisions.

1 YOU

And the last, and most important, bit of advice is just be yourself. Don't try to copy others, and don't think you're worse than anyone else. Try new sports and clubs, start speaking new languages, make new friends, meet some great new teachers… all of that and more. But stay true to who you are. After all, there's only one of you!

I AM Cooool

SUMMER HOLIDAY READING!

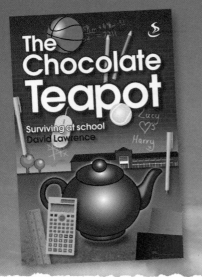

THE CHOCOLATE TEAPOT: SURVIVING AT SCHOOL

by David Lawrence

What's the worst possible way to start secondary school? Should you kick bullies? What if all your friends swear, and you can't do the maths test? What about girlfriends/boyfriends? Just as importantly, are teachers human?! *Health warning:* this book might make you laugh. If it doesn't, you're probably dead, or at least very seriously ill!

£4.99

9781844270514

FRIENDS FIRST

by Claire Pedrick and Andy Morgan

Friends First takes a look at relationships and how confusing they can get: friendship groups, best friends, girlfriends, boyfriends, and even being friends with your parents! This book will help you untangle these relationships and think about big issues like peer pressure, flirting, going to church and what to do about bullying in a way that makes sense to YOUR life.

£4.99

9781844275038

Available from your local Christian bookshop or **www.scriptureunion.org.uk/shop**.

Big questions

781 children in the UK about to move on to secondary school were asked these three big questions. What would your answers be?

What will you miss most about your old school?

The history

What is the scariest thing about your new school?

Year 6s

What is the best thing about your new school?

Teachers

On the next few pages you'll find the most common responses to these questions. Check to see if your answers are in the top ten!

I like the idea of mixing children up from different schools in forms because it gives other children chances to get to know each other!

I'm excited about the new playground and getting to know more about the new friends I'm going to meet.

The thing that makes me nervous are the sixth-formers – they're so much taller and older than us!

Thanks to the children from Balvanich Primary (Isle of Benbecula); Cairnshill Primary (S Belfast); Coppull St John's Primary (Lancashire); Gibson Primary (Omagh); Gilnow Primary (Bolton); Hillview Primary (Hucclecote, Gloucester); Kingsland School (Bangor, N Ireland); Loughton Middle School (Milton Keynes); Mellor Primary (Leicester); many Nottinghamshire Primary Schools who know Nick Harding!; St Anthony's RC Primary (Watford); St John's C of E Primary (Sparkhill, Birmingham); St John's C of E Primary (Brinscall, Lancashire); St John's C of E Primary (Whittle-le-Woods, Lancashire); St Joseph's RC Primary School (Carryduff, N Ireland); St Mary's C of E Primary (Kirtbury, W Berks); Swanbourne House School (Milton Keynes).

what will you miss most about your old school?

Easy work 3%

Teachers and dinner ladies 31%

Sport 4%

Being the oldest 2%

Staying in your class, smallness of school 2%

Responsibility 1%

Friends 51

Food 3%

Art/drama 1%

Fun things like discos, concerts… 2%

Year 6 was the best year! I'm going to miss so much!

What is the scariest thing about your new school?

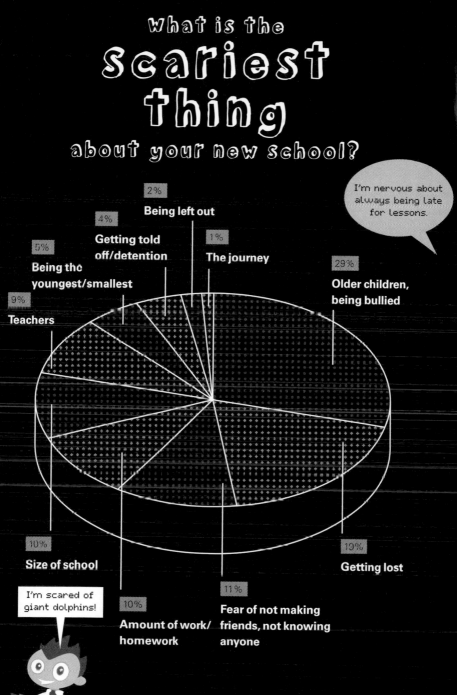

- 2% — Being left out
- 4% — Getting told off/detention
- 1% — The journey
- 5% — Being the youngest/smallest
- 29% — Older children, being bullied
- 9% — Teachers
- 10% — Size of school
- 10% — Amount of work/homework
- 11% — Fear of not making friends, not knowing anyone
- 19% — Getting lost

I'm nervous about always being late for lessons.

I'm scared of giant dolphins!

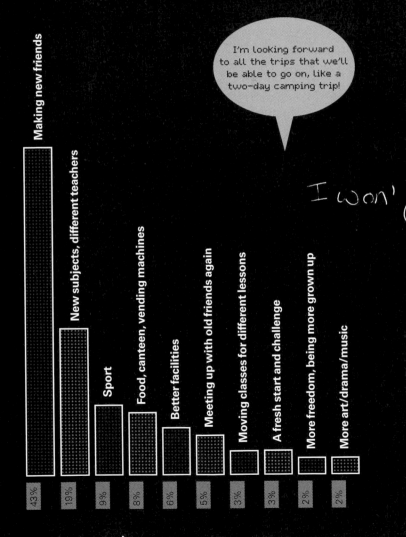

Mad lit

Have you ever been told that you're a poet – you just didn't know it?
Here's your chance to make up your own poem, DIY-style, by filling in the gaps below.
Don't worry about rhyming or anything, just express yourself!

My old school is ___great___ (description),

I'll ___cry___ (action) on the last day

When I see ___everyone___ (person or thing) for the last time,

___Goodbye___ (saying) is what I'll say

I'll be ___sad___ (emotion) the first time

I ___cry___ (action) on my own

But _____ (person, thing or action) has made me feel

_____ (emotion) about the unknown

I know I'll be _____ (emotion)

when _____ (thing or event) ends

I can't wait for _____ (event or place), where I'll meet

_____ (description) friends!

Brain-scrambling wordsearch

C	H	I	P	S	H	T	A	M	A	X	E
L	U	N	C	H	T	I	M	E	I	M	T
A	L	M	F	O	O	T	B	A	L	L	E
S	I	L	R	C	F	M	S	R	A	I	X
S	C	E	I	K	R	O	E	T	P	B	T
R	N	S	E	E	C	C	W	T	R	B	
O	E	S	N	N	A	O	V	O	A	O	
O	P	O	D	I	C	N	N	N	P	R	O
M	G	N	S	O	H	T	D	N	U	Y	K
R	E	L	U	R	T	E	A	C	H	E	R
P	T	R	A	I	N	E	R	S	U	B	P
S	C	H	O	O	L	N	Y	K	O	O	B

Can you see what phrase is made up of the letters that are left over?
Write them down here in the order they appear.

_ _ ' _ _ _ _ _ _ _ _ _ _ !

Can you find all these words in the grid?

Art
Book
Bus
Canteen
Chips
Classroom
Exam
Football
French
Friends
Hockey
Homework
Laptop
Lesson
Library
Lunchtime
Maths
Pen
Pencil
Ruler
School
Secondary
Teacher
Textbook
Trainers

I've found chips!
Mmm, chips...

Beat bullying

Amy Stock works for schoolswork.co.uk, a website that gives lots of help to people who work in schools. She's got some wise words on a tricky subject!

OK, so let's be real. One of the things that scares most of us about moving up to secondary school is the thought of bullying. Why does it bother us so much? Does it really matter what others think or do?

Actually, the fear of being laughed at, hurt or totally ignored is a big deal for a lot of us, and it's OK to admit that.

We can't control what other people do, but we can control what we do about it, so it's worth taking some time to think this stuff through ahead of time.

There are three ways to beat bullying…

1 Be strong in who you are

Remember that you *are* different from everyone else – it's a fact! So if you do things differently to others it means that you're just being yourself, and that's great! Don't deny who you are, and if someone tells you that you're different, remind them in a friendly way that they are too. They'll soon get bored and get the message that you're confident and strong in who you are.

2 Make friends from day one

Don't be afraid to say hi to people right from the start. Everyone else is as nervous as you are (however confident they might look!) and the sooner you get talking to people and making friends, the less likely you are to be a target for bullies.

3 Speak up

If something happens to you, remember it is your right to be treated fairly, so speak up! It may not feel like the best idea, but there will be someone you can talk to – whether a friend, peer mentor, your form tutor or a relative. Please don't stay silent; you and your feelings are very important!

Visit **www.bbclic.com** for more ideas, support and stories.

Quizzical
quandaries

How ready are you for your new school?
Try these dilemmas and find out!

1

On your second day at school you get horribly lost. You have no idea where you are and you're already late for your first maths lesson at your new school. Do you…?

a) Ask a passing Year 11 where your maths classroom is.

b) Hide in the loos and cry.

c) Decide to find the classroom for the lesson after maths instead; at least you won't be late for that one.

d) Find a teacher, explain that you're lost and ask for help.

2

You see someone you know from your primary school being pushed around by some Year 9 lads. Do you…?

a) Walk on by, as if you didn't know them.

b) Wade in, fists flying, to try and even up the fight.

c) Ask an adult in school to sort it out.

d) Stand and watch, shouting 'Fight, fight!'

3

By the end of your first week in school, you've been given way more homework than you're used to getting, and by Sunday night you haven't completed everything. Do you…?

a) See what homework needs to be done for Monday and make sure that's finished.

b) Panic and only manage to finish your art homework – a masterpiece you call 'Stress'.

c) Text your friend to see if you can copy theirs.

d) Give up completely and prepare yourself to be told off every lesson for a week.

> Use a bit of common sense – it's easy!

4

A friend from primary school is acting as if they don't want to know you any more. Do you…?

a) Keep texting them. They must have run out of credit.

b) Confront them angrily about why they're ignoring you.

c) Talk to them about it. They may have just moved on.

d) Freeze them out in revenge. Two can play at that game.

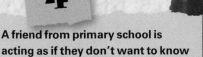

What's your score?

Find out how many points your answers are worth, add them all together and then see what you've scored!

1 a) 5   b) 2   c) 1   d) 8

2 a) 2   b) 1   c) 8   d) 1

3 a) 8   b) 4   c) 2   d) 1

4 a) 4   b) 2   c) 8   d) 1

5 a) 5   b) 2   c) 2   d) 8

What happens if you don't have any?!

5

After two weeks of being at secondary school, a new friend keeps calling you the wrong name. Do you…?

a) Make yourself a badge, saying 'Hi, my name's [your actual name]!'

b) Shout, 'That's not my name!' loudly in their face, the next time they call you the wrong name.

c) Tell your form tutor than the person is bullying you by calling you the wrong name.

d) Gently remind them of your name the next time they get it wrong.

If you got:

0–11 points – Hmmm… you could do with thinking about things a bit more before moving up. Maybe talking to a teacher, parent, carer or someone from church might help you figure out what secondary school is really going to be like.

12–21 points – You're getting there but there's a little way to go yet before you make the move. Try reading a bit more of *It's Your Move!* to get some valuable tips.

22–31 points – You're almost ready! Make sure you read every last bit of *It's Your Move!* so you're well prepared for secondary school.

32–40 points – Well done! You've clearly been paying attention and you're all ready to go! Enjoy secondary school – you'll be fine.

You know me!

You have looked deep into my heart, LORD,
and you know all about me.
You know when I am resting or when I am working,
and from heaven you discover my thoughts.

You notice everything I do and everywhere I go.
Before I even speak a word,
you know what I will say,
and with your powerful arm
you protect me from every side.
I can't understand all of this!
Such wonderful knowledge is far above me.

This poem is found in the Bible, in a section called the Psalms ('psalm' means 'song'). It was probably written by a man called King David, who lived around 3,000 years ago. He had a very exciting, but often dangerous, life. Yet he knew he could rely on God, because God knew everything about him, and loved him.

Look at the poem again. Underline in green all the words or phrases that you like. Underline in red all the words or phrases that surprise you. Put a big blue question mark next to anything you don't understand!

Where could I go to escape
from your Spirit or from your sight?
If I were to climb up to the highest heavens,
you would be there.
If I were to dig down to the world of the dead
you would also be there.

Suppose I had wings like the dawning day
and flew across the ocean.
Even then your powerful arm would guide and protect me.
Or suppose I said, I'll hide in the dark
until night comes to cover me over.
But you see in the dark
because daylight and dark are all the same to you.

Psalm 139: 1–12

Are there any questions you want to ask about this poem? If you've got a question, write it here:

There may be someone at your school who can help you answer your question.

Does this poem help you as you think about going to your new school?

what a picture!

When you move to your new school, you'll meet lots of great people, but you don't want to forget your old friends and teachers, do you? Why not take some photographs, print them off and stick them in here, so you can look back at them later.

Spot the really important missing object...

Oh no! You spent ages last night carefully packing your school bag and this morning you find your annoying little sister has been messing with your stuff. See how many differences you can spot between the two pictures.

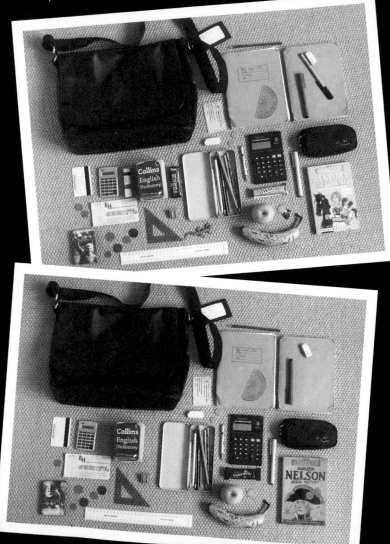

A DEADLY SECRET

by Robert Harrison

* * *

Jonathan was very scared. He didn't know what to say, and he didn't know what not to say.

The tall Roman centurion was staring at him. Jonathan smiled weakly at the man and then looked down at the engravings on the soldier's polished armour. He had never been this close to a Roman before. Sometimes he and his friends dared each other to run up behind a Roman soldier in the street and tap the backplate of his armour. Once or twice his friends had been rewarded with a sharp jab from the blunt end of the soldier's spear. But standing right next to one in a dark corridor was quite another matter. Jonathan kept a close eye on the man's short, flat sword, and wondered how many people it had killed.

Whenever Jonathan went out into the city on his own, his mum always told him, 'Keep away from the Romans, and keep out of trouble.'

Since his Uncle Paul had been arrested by the Romans, she was even more concerned. Now he was right in the middle of trouble – serious trouble. And Jonathan was standing outside the door of the top Roman commander in all Jerusalem.

You haven't done anything wrong, Jonathan reminded himself. But even though that was true, he still felt guilty.

'Just say what you overheard,' had been his Uncle Paul's advice. But Jonathan was not convinced. It would be much safer to say nothing. He had only told his teacher in the first place because the plot concerned his own mum's brother. His teacher had said he would have to tell Uncle Paul, and Uncle Paul had insisted that he tell the commander. So here he was, right beside a fully armed soldier, in the barracks where Uncle Paul was a prisoner.

If that gang finds out it was me who dobbed on them, he warned his already frightened self, they'll kill me too.

Jonathan looked up at the centurion. It was too late to run away. He was almost as safely locked inside the barracks as his uncle. (Paul was chained to a stone pillar in the guard room.)

The commander's door opened silently. A dark-haired gentleman in a white toga invited him in. Was this the commander? Jonathan didn't know. He had never actually seen Commander Claudius, although he had heard plenty about him; everyone in Jerusalem hated the man.

'Sir,' the centurion said, 'the prisoner, Paul, asked me to bring this young man to you. He has something to tell you.'

The dark-haired man was the commander.

The centurion shut the door and stood in front of it, his hand on his sword. Now Jonathan had no chance of escape, and no one to help him. He was frightened of the Romans; he was terrified of the gang that was planning to kill his uncle. He would have to decide by himself what to say, and what not to say.

Commander Claudius stepped into the middle of the room and studied him. Jonathan tried to look into his eyes, but he couldn't. He looked at the floor. The commander spoke. His voice was friendly – not at all what Jonathan had expected.

'What's your name, young man?'

'Jonathan,' he mumbled, still looking at the floor.

'Why did you come to see Paul?'

Jonathan looked up at the man. 'He's my uncle.'

He quickly looked down to the floor again. Be careful, he warned himself, if you say too much you could land yourself in even more trouble.

Commander Claudius reached out a strong arm and took Jonathan's hand. He led him to the window and crouched down so that their eyes were at the same level.

'Now,' he said softly, so the centurion couldn't hear, 'what is it you want to tell me?'

Want to tell you? Jonathan thought with a rush of panic. I don't want to tell you anything!

His mum's voice echoed up into his mind: Keep away from the Romans, Jon. It was way too late for that!

He wondered what his friends would say if they could see him now. They would say, Never trust a Roman. That was what everyone in Jerusalem said.

But the grey eyes of Commander Claudius said the opposite. They said, It's all right, you can trust me.

The commander let go of Jonathan's hand and gazed out of the window. Jonathan relaxed, just a little. The window looked across to the huge stone wall of the Temple. It was there that Uncle Paul had been arrested. It was there that Jonathan had overheard some of the Jewish extremists plotting to kill him. And it was in that very street, between the barracks and the Temple, that they were waiting to ambush him and kill him, because they hated Paul for his belief in Jesus.

Jonathan knew he had to say something. Paul's life depended on it. Ten minutes ago, Uncle Paul had looked at Jonathan with his dark, piercing eyes and said, 'Just tell the commander what you heard.' It had seemed such simple advice when he said it. But now that Jonathan was on his own, he didn't know what to do.

Commander Claudius turned round and looked at him. 'What do you want to tell me?' He emphasised the want, and it unlocked Jonathan's indecision.

He decided to say everything. He was just about to start when all the muddled fears of his upbringing surged into his mind, shouting: You can't trust the Romans!

He was stuck again.

A favourite phrase of Uncle Paul's floated into his thoughts. Whatever happens, thank God. Not knowing what else to do, Jonathan felt that he should give it a try.

'Almighty God,' he prayed above the confusion in his thoughts, 'thank you. Thank you … that this Roman … is a kind man. I didn't think he would be. Amen.'

Almost immediately the storm in Jonathan's head was calmed. It was quite clear to him what he should do.

'The religious leaders are going to ask you to take my Uncle Paul back to their Council,' he told the commander. 'They will say that they need to ask him more questions.'

The man nodded, inviting him to continue.

'Don't do it,' Jonathan said, with more confidence than he thought possible. 'A gang of more than forty men is going to ambush him. They have vowed not to eat or drink anything until Uncle Paul is dead.' He paused. Had he said everything? Not quite. 'It's all arranged,' he added. 'The only thing they need is for you to take him down the road.'

The commander stood upright. ' I thank you,' he said politely. 'I will have Paul taken to a safe place tonight.'

Then he looked out of his window at the street below. A smile crept across his face. Jonathan had never seen a Roman smile. It quite surprised him.

'Somewhere down there,' Claudius said with a slightly mischievous chuckle, 'there are going to be forty very hungry and very thirsty men.'

This story is from the book of Acts, chapter 23, in the Bible.
What do you think you would have done in Jonathan's situation?

Dooooooooodling

OK – we know you love doodling on your schoolbooks, so here's a place where you can doodle to your heart's content without getting told off! What's on your mind as you think about secondary school? Put it on paper!

2
cool
4
School!

M
4
E

2 Cool 4 School!

2 Pretty

Flower Power

Flower Power

Get your pens out and get doodling!

Fill in these columns with your top three…

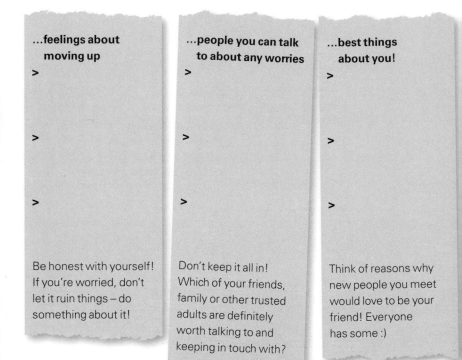

…feelings about moving up

>

>

>

Be honest with yourself! If you're worried, don't let it ruin things – do something about it!

…people you can talk to about any worries

>

>

>

Don't keep it all in! Which of your friends, family or other trusted adults are definitely worth talking to and keeping in touch with?

…best things about you!

>

>

>

Think of reasons why new people you meet would love to be your friend! Everyone has some :)

Use the space here to doodle or write things that you're really looking forward to doing (or being allowed to do!) as you move up to secondary school.

Growing Up

Boys' page
No girls allowed!

What are you thinking?

So, what do you want to say, now that there are no girls around? Are you looking forward to going to secondary school? Or are you a bit nervous? Here are some words that might describe how you feel. Circle the ones that match how you feel. Write your own thoughts as well if you want to.

Excited **Nervous** Happy

Too much to think about **Can't wait**

Not bothered **Don't want to go**

Bored Sad Scared **Worried**

Why do you feel that way about your new school? Do you still have questions about your move? It's OK to be sad or worried; we all feel that way about new things. But don't let it take over. Find an adult you trust – it could be a parent, carer, teacher, someone from your church or sports club – and talk to them about your questions or worries.

Great stuff to do

You'll get the chance to do some great new stuff when you get to your new school. You might take up a musical instrument, join the football team or learn to play chess! Graffiti this space with what you fancy getting stuck into!

It's like a maze!

Can you find your way to all the classrooms in the correct order without crossing your own path?

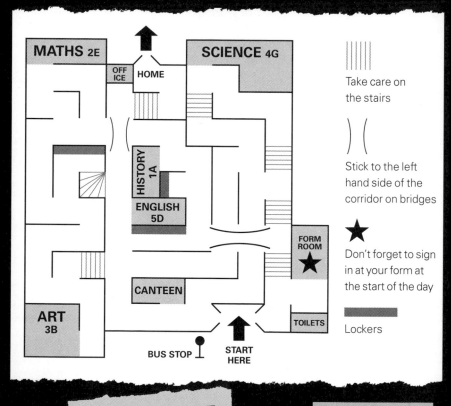

‖‖‖‖	Take care on the stairs
) (	Stick to the left hand side of the corridor on bridges
★	Don't forget to sign in at your form at the start of the day
▬▬	Lockers

Registration
1st period: History 1A
2nd period: Maths 2E
3rd period: Art 3B
Lunch
4th period: Science 4G
5th period: English 5D
Home time!

If you get lost, just ask someone!

JEALOUS BROTHERS

by Robert Harrison

* * *

'One day my brothers will bow down to me,' Joseph told himself as he walked through the fields to meet them.

Joseph's dad had sent him to check up on his older brothers and their sheep. Joseph knew what would happen when he found them. They would tease him, bully him, push him and slap him. They always did. They hated him. But Joseph had had a dream. He had dreamt it twice: in one dream some stars bowed down to him – one star for each brother; another time it was the bundles of corn that his brothers had just harvested. Somehow, Joseph knew that these dreams came from God.

He had ten brothers, all older than him. They were half-brothers, the children of his dad's other wives. But his dad loved Joseph's mum more than the others; everyone knew that. His dad told everyone how special Joseph was and had even given him an expensive embroidered coat. That's why his brothers hated him. They were jealous.

Joseph climbed to the top of another hill. His magnificent coat billowed in the wind. Its gold and silver threads sparkling in the sunlight reminded him of the stars in his dream. His brothers were below him in the valley, with their sheep. Joseph watched them for a while, imagining all ten of them on their knees in front of him.

When the brothers saw Joseph, they huddled together. They were talking about him. He was suddenly afraid. Simeon was doing the talking, and he was the worst of the lot. They were planning something bad; he could feel it.

Reuben, the oldest, walked away from the group. He had obviously disagreed with them. Reuben was the sensible one. The other brothers stopped talking and walked up towards Joseph.

Joseph's heart was thumping. There were none of the usual insults. The brothers were silent. They wanted to hurt him – he could see it in their faces. He turned and ran – up the hill. The brothers chased him. They were older, stronger, and faster. As he scrambled up the rocky hillside, Joseph remembered his dream. One day these hateful brothers would bow to him.

What a stupid time to think that! he told himself. He concentrated on running. They were close now. Strong hands grabbed him.

'Reuben!' Joseph shouted.

His eldest brother was sulking in the valley.

Joseph tried a scream. 'REUBEN!'

Reuben climbed towards them. 'I told you not to hurt the boy,' he called.

'We're not going to hurt him,' Simeon mocked. 'We're going to kill him. And I'm having that coat.'

Simeon tugged at Joseph's collar. There were so many hands gripping his arms and legs that he couldn't move. Reuben was shouting for them to stop.

The brothers wrestled the precious coat off Joseph, letting out a wild cheer when it was finally free. Simeon stood up, pulled it round his own shoulders, and danced a stupid dance. Reuben walked away.

Joseph's dream still nagged at his mind. They'll bow down to you, Joseph, it seemed to say.

'No they won't,' he replied in his thoughts. 'They're about to kill me!'

Simeon stopped dancing and said coldly, 'Let's do it.'

Joseph's heart sank. Strong arms lifted him off the ground and carried him off. He wriggled and kicked and twisted. 'Don't kill me,' he pleaded. 'Please don't kill me.'

'Shut up!' Simeon snapped.

'Hit me,' Joseph begged, desperate to distract them from anything worse. 'Hit me as hard as you can.'

'We will if you don't shut up,' Simeon warned.

That was what Joseph hoped for. Wild with panic he shouted, 'Come on then, weaklings, hit me. Hurt me.'

'Here it is,' Simeon announced.

Whatever Joseph's brothers had planned was about to happen. He was about to die. He screamed. This was the end. He was falling, falling into darkness. His brothers cheered. He remembered his dream. Then... Thud!

Joseph was alone; it was totally dark. His back hurt, his head ached. He was surrounded by silence.

'Hello?' he called out. His voice echoed around him. 'Help!' he shouted louder. He crawled around and worked out that he was in an empty water storage cistern. He tried to climb the walls but they were too smooth. He felt for a puddle of water that he could drink. There wasn't one.

He cried. There was nothing else to do. He couldn't climb out. No one could hear him. He was going to die.

A vivid image flared up in his mind. The sun and moon and eleven stars were bowing down to him. It was his dream. Joseph was angry. His dream was useless; it had caused all this trouble. He ignored it and thought about his mum: she was expecting a baby. Maybe it would be a brother – a real brother. His dream fought back. He felt strangely calm. The dream swept away his fear. He knew it was from God. He would get out of this cistern. His brothers would bow down to him.

The lid to the cistern scraped open. Light poured in. A face appeared. 'It's your lucky day, dream boy.' Simeon's voice was cruel. He threw down a rope and told Joseph to tie it round himself. Other faces appeared – strange faces.

'What's happening?' he shouted anxiously.

Simeon laughed. 'We've done a deal with some Ishmaelites,' he replied.

Ishmaelites! The Ishmaelites were their enemies; there was an ancient feud between the tribes. Joseph's dream flooded back into his mind. 'Trust me,' it told him.

The rope tightened and lifted Joseph off the floor.

'Trust me,' the voice in his mind said as he swung helplessly in the darkness.

Hands heaved Joseph out into the light, but the rope kept pulling. It was dragging him along the ground. Sharp stones were ripping and tearing his skin. A stick crashed across his back. 'Get up, you fool!' a voice shouted. Joseph struggled to his feet. The rope was attached to a camel, and the camel was following a long line of other camels. Where were they taking him?

He looked back at his brothers. Simeon waved a large purse of money and shouted, 'Goodbye, Joseph. Sweet dreams!'

They had sold him. He was being taken to Egypt as a slave...

Read what happened next in the Bible, from the book of Genesis, chapters 39 to 45.

Joseph was taken into a scary and unfamiliar situation, but God was with him, keeping him safe every step of the way. In the end, Joseph worked his way up from being a household slave to being the Prime Minister of all Egypt, and God used him to save many people from famine.

When they all met up again later on in the story, God's promise through Joseph's dream came true and Joseph's brothers did indeed bow down to the important person he had become. Joseph was able to forgive them, saying, 'You tried to harm me, but God made it turn out for the best, so that he could save all these people...' (Genesis 50:20).

Designer duds

What would your perfect school uniform look like?
Use this space to design your very own secondary school stylings.

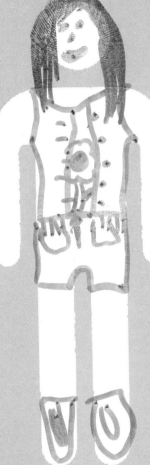

it's my move

**JOEL BROWN
YEAR 6
ST JOSEPH'S PRIMARY
GATESHEAD**

I'm looking forward to spending some more time on art!

What are you going to miss about St Joseph's?

It is quite a small school so I know everyone in the whole school and the teachers know everyone individually. I will also miss the friends I have made there.

What worries you about going to secondary school?

The fact that there is going to be heaps of homework. Making new friends because I am the only one from my primary school going to St Thomas More. It is a huge school and there will be lots of new stuff to get used to.

What are you looking forward to?

The range of subjects – for example, we could not dissect things in science at primary school but I am hoping we can at St Thomas More! The freedom to choose what I do.

**ROKSANA TABOR
YEAR 6
ST ETHELBERT'S
CATHOLIC PRIMARY
SCHOOL SLOUGH**

I will miss my best friends Gabriela and Kasia because they aren't going with me to secondary school. Just one person is going to the same school as me – she's called Jemma and we are going to art school. Yes I am happy about it but maybe she will be in a different class and have different friends. I'm looking forward to meeting new friends and learning more at my new school.

Despite the worries I have about moving to secondary school, it is great to know that God will always be with me, as he was at primary school.

Pg. 9
Bits and

Can its shap
be changed

lid

can it

49

Do u hve a pencil I cou bom

> I felt loads better after my induction day!

**THOMAS LINGARD
YEAR 6
ST BERNADETTE'S
CATHOLIC PRIMARY
SCHOOL
MILTON KEYNES**

> I am looking forward to starting new subjects and also having different meals for lunch such as pizza, chips and burgers!

**SOPHIE ANDERSON
YEAR 6**

Secondary school is huge, I'll say that! But just because it's huge, that doesn't mean you have anything to be scared about. After you've been to your induction day, you usually feel a lot better, as I did. While you're there, the teachers and other students will answer most questions you may have. The induction day really helped me get control of my nerves.

I'll probably miss the fun free time we get at the end of a Friday afternoon. A lot of my friends are going to the same school as me, but that doesn't mean I'll have a better time than others because at secondary school you have to make new friends.

At secondary school you get a lot of privileges that you don't get in primary school, such as the freedom between lessons. That's what I'm looking forward to.

**JOACHIM BONDOY
YEAR 6**

None of my friends are going to the same school as me, but I don't mind because I want to make new friends and start over again, and I feel fine about that. I am looking forward to seeing what it will be like when I move!

Don't be worried about secondary school, just relax and keep cool!

I will always miss my friends and teachers as they have been really supportive and helpful. Secondary school will be hard as I am not used to the building, teachers and friends. I am nervous about forgetting my books as I will have more responsibility. I am going to have to be more independent as my mum can't run around after me

I am sure there will always be something to look forward to, whether it's sport, drama or a specific subject. I am really looking forward to doing more sport than was offered at primary school, with qualified teachers to do your favourite sport. There are never enough girls to complete a girl's football team at my primary school and I know there is a girl's team at Burnham Grammar School.

I am looking forward to going on my own by train as it is a new experience.

**LYDIA SEWELL
YEAR 6
RYVERS PRIMARY
SLOUGH**

The visiting teachers made me realise secondary school won't be so different.

LUCY CLARK
YEAR 6
RICKLEY PARK PRIMARY SCHOOL
MILTON KEYNES

I'm worried about wearing a tie for the first time!

SIMRAN GHOTRA
YEAR 6

Going to secondary school can make your head spin and make you feel out of control. New opportunities bring a sense of excitement too – science labs, art rooms and trips abroad.

I do feel prepared, we've had lots of lessons about moving up and some of the teachers came over and taught us English. We've got an induction day planned and some older children came in and spoke positively about their experiences. All this has made me realise the teachers aren't so different, the other children aren't that different and there are no more bullies at secondary school than anywhere else.

Yes I have some doubts about going to a school that is four times bigger… but this is a whole new chapter in my life and I intend to enjoy it!

I didn't get my first choice.

KARL HEMINGWAY
RICKMANSWORTH

Karl had to take an entrance exam to decide which secondary school he would go to. He was nervous before the exam but he talked with God and that helped him. Unfortunately he was very disappointed when he didn't get into his first choice school.

However, he says, 'I'm now glad I went to Rickmansworth School and I wonder why I worried so much. Look at it like this – going to secondary school is like a big adventure just waiting for you!'

I was home schooled!

My dad's a teacher!

ISOBEL O'NEIL
ARDVASAR, SCOTLAND
GOING INTO S1 AT
PLOCKTON HIGH SCHOOL

I live on the Isle of Skye and I've just finished 'the O'Neil's Primary School.' I was home schooled, with my younger brother, taught by my Mum. Plockton is about 30 miles from my house.

I've already spent a week at the High School which was quite good. I was really nervous at first, not knowing any other children there and not knowing what to expect. It's a big thing to go to a school of 300 having been taught at home. On the first day I didn't enjoy it because it was so different to what I was used to, but the rest of the week I loved it. I met a couple of people but I want to make new friends in the first term..

I'm going with my Dad because he's a teacher at Plockton. I'll get him for Business Management and it was strange during my induction week to have him as a teacher. I have to ignore that he's my Dad. I'm not nervous about that and it's helpful to have him there so I know somebody.

My family and lots of people at my church are encouraging me not to be nervous because God's with me. I'm still nervous about starting school but it helps a little bit, and I'm actually looking forward to it.

JACK BICKNELL
YEAR 6
STYAL PRIMARY
STOCKPORT

I am nervous about:

> Meeting the Headmistress – as I've not yet met her
> The extra homework
> The fact that the school is SO big – my primary school only had 100 children!
> The fact that it's a whole new experience and I'm not sure exactly what to expect…

I am excited about:

> Meeting my form tutor again – as I've already met her on the open day
> Meeting my new classmates
> The food! Already tasted it on an open day and it's delicious (compared to my primary school) – much better variety
> Getting stuck into the sports

I survived!

I was worried about making friends and fitting in, but I soon realised that everyone else was feeling like that too!

FREYA STRANGWAYS
YEAR 7
MILTON KEYNES

Before I moved from Year 6 to Year 7, I was very worried about making friends and not fitting in, but when I started at my new school I realised that everyone else was feeling like that too! We all wanted to make friends, and being open and friendly with others will help you make friends quickly. Just be yourself.

What I like best about my secondary school is that there are so many people, which means you can make lots more friends! I also like that there is a bigger range of subjects to learn about.

My advice to you is to be yourself and be open and friendly towards people. With teachers, it is easiest to just listen, because they don't like you interrupting or being disruptive. Usually you will be given a list of equipment that you need. Each night before you go to bed, check that you have all the books and equipment for the next day, and that you have done your homework, so you don't have to rush in the morning.

When I moved schools I was worried about finding my way around the huge school I was moving to. When I arrived at school, we were all in the same position, so if I wasn't moving in a group, there was always someone I could ask for directions.

MATTHEW BOASE
YEAR 7

54

Introducing Sequences

Numbers, letters or sym[...] [...]ther to form a pattern.

RAHUL KAKAIYA
YEAR 7
ST BERNARD'S CATHOLIC GRAMMAR
SLOUGH

I love the canteen and getting to throw wet sponges at teachers for charity!

My primary school was the best; I had loads of friends, fun lessons and just generally loved it! Until high school, or so I thought… Back then I thought no one would like me, I would have no friends and it would be a living hell!

So on my first day, it was hard to find new friends, which was natural. I think I was also one of only five other people that did not have any kids from their old school there. Surprisingly, in the second week or so, I found myself with a group of friends who were really nice to me.

I think the best bits of high school so far are the canteen (I hated my primary school one), the charity events like sponging teachers and students, and the lessons and teachers.

Even though I am loving high school, I cannot deny that I still miss my friends from my primary school. That's why we meet up really regularly, and most of the time I don't miss them as much as I thought I would.

JOSHUA READ
YEAR 7
LIVERPOOL

The advice I would give to Year 6s is to do your homework the day you get it, not the night before it is due in!

Apple

> I can always trust my Head of Year to be there for me!

> I really enjoyed going away with my new classmates to get to know them better.

SHANNON O'BRIEN
YEAR 7
SLOUGH

PETER CAMERON
YEAR 7
NORTHERN IRELAND

I found it easier than I expected to move from Primary School to Secondary School. I expected to get lost quite a lot and be late for my lessons, but it turns out I wasn't even late for any of them!

The teachers at our school are very caring and they always make sure I'm happy and help me at bad times. When you start secondary school, you will have a form tutor who you will have for the whole time in your secondary school, and you also have a head of year. Heads of year are very friendly and really kind and helpful. When I get upset, I go to my head of year, 'cause I know she will cheer me up!

I was really worried about not being able to find my way around or getting crushed in the corridor when everyone was changing classes. But it was ok because there is a system of moving around by walking on one side of the corridor, so I didn't need to worry.

I really enjoyed going on a residential with my classmates. It was a great way to get to know the rest of the class, and when we went back to school we all knew each other better and got on well.

The best thing about my secondary school is that each subject lasts only 35 minutes so you know that soon you are going to move on. This really helps in subjects you don't like much!

My advice would be to try to get organised and remember what you need each day. Join in with after-school activities to get to know more people who like the same things you do.

BETHANY LANE
GLENELG

**BOTH IN S1
(FIRST YEAR SECONDARY)
AT PLOCKTON HIGH
SCHOOL, IN ROSS-SHIRE,
SCOTLAND.**

ALASTAIR SHILLAKER
KISHORN

When you moved up to High School, did you have any worries?

Bethany: I was worried about getting lost because it's much bigger than Glenelg Primary, and I was worried I would get on the wrong bus. There's about six buses that go to different places. It takes about an hour and a half so I get the bus at half seven in the morning. It's 26 miles to school.

What have been the best bits of High School?

Alastair: Making new friends, which I did. One my best friends lives in Nostie which is 24 miles from my house.

Bethany: It's bigger and there's more people, so you're not stuck with the same people your whole life. There's more stuff like Home Ec. where you get to cook stuff and more teachers. That's good because they all have different opinions. I like English and Art and Music where I can get involved.

What advice would you give someone moving up to High School?

Alastair: I would tell them not to be worried, and if you are worried about bullying, like I was, there are people around who would be glad to help. Knowing God has helped me to hang around with the right people and also not to swear like others. That gets them into trouble but I don't.

Bethany: If you're a bit worried about things, you can go to God for guidance. Nobody really minds at Plockton because there's lots of people who are into God and we get lots of support from Christian clubs and Dave the youth worker.

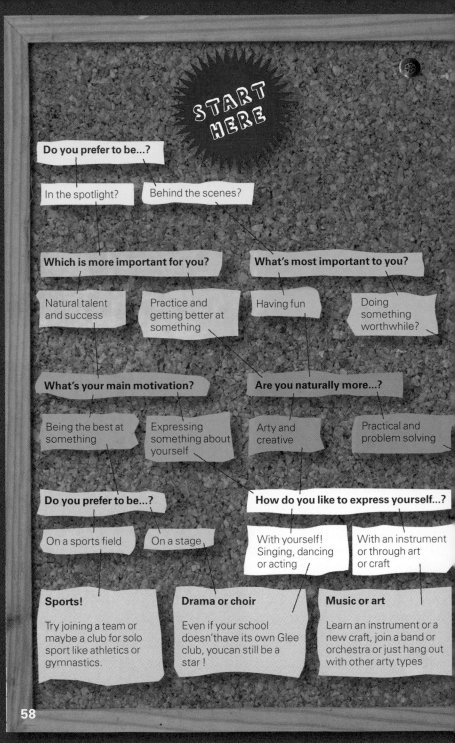

START HERE

Do you prefer to be...?

In the spotlight? Behind the scenes?

Which is more important for you?

Natural talent and success

Practice and getting better at something

What's most important to you?

Having fun

Doing something worthwhile?

What's your main motivation?

Being the best at something

Expressing something about yourself

Are you naturally more...?

Arty and creative

Practical and problem solving

Do you prefer to be...?

On a sports field On a stage

How do you like to express yourself...?

With yourself! Singing, dancing or acting

With an instrument or through art or craft

Sports!

Try joining a team or maybe a club for solo sport like athletics or gymnastics.

Drama or choir

Even if your school doesn't have its own Glee club, you can still be a star!

Music or art

Learn an instrument or a new craft, join a band or orchestra or just hang out with other arty types

WHICH CLUBS TO JOIN?

After-school or lunchtime clubs are a great way to get to know people and make new friends who have similar interests to yours. When you move up to secondary school, you'll probably have a much bigger choice of activities! If you need help to decide what to do, try this fun quiz…

Are you more interested in...?

Things going on around the world

Local news and happenings

What do you like to talk about with your friends...?

The future – what's going to happen next

What happened yesterday

When you hear about something going on, do you prefer to...?

Tell others about it

Get involved yourself

Maths/science/ computer club

Lessons not quite exciting enough? Discover new things with like-minded friends

School newspaper/ website

Get in the know with all the latest news and work together with other cool people

School forum/council

Serve your fellow school mates by getting involved with the important issues

MEET THE TEACHERS

Name: Ian Butt
School: St Paul's Catholic School
Subject: RE
Likes: Cricket, football (Walsall FC!), films, TV, PS3 gaming
Favourite food: Chinese takeaway (to be specific, crispy duck, sweet and sour chicken Hong Kong style, egg fried rice and pancake rolls!!)

Top teacher tips
> Do your homework the night it is set.
> Be yourself and ignore anyone who doesn't like that.
> Remember you'll never get a single school day back in your life, so take advantage of every opportunity. Make each day count.

Words of wisdom
School is an excellent preparation for the rest of your life. You'll have to do some things you enjoy, some things you don't, some things you're naturally good at and some things you're not and you'll come into contact with some people you like and some you don't. In 20 years time you definitely WON'T wish you'd put less effort into learning at school, but if you don't do your best, you almost certainly WILL wish you had tried harder.

First day at secondary school (as a teacher!)
On my first day as a teacher, I stood at 9am in the corridor waiting, terrified, for my first class to arrive. An experienced teacher across the corridor said to me 'Don't worry... they're far more scared than you are.' After one lesson with that class, I have to say she was wrong!

Memorable moment
One Christmas, the headteacher found out I was a Christian, so asked me to do the Christmas assembly to all 250 Year 11 pupils! After much thought I began the assembly by taking out a can of lager and starting to drink it… That got their attention! I went on to talk about how, for many people, all that Christmas means is an excuse for parties and drinking. But for Christians it's about celebrating that Jesus is with us – something that is helpful to remember in school whether you are a pupil or teacher, all year round.

Key for co-or
ive co-ordinates in alphabetical

Name: Anna Williams
School: RSA Academy, near Dudley, West Midlands
Subject: Music
Claim to fame: I've met Karl Kennedy from *Neighbours*
Favourite food: Melt-in-the-middle chocolate puddings (they are so good I usually have to lick the plate after finishing!)

First day at secondary school

My school didn't have a uniform, so on my first day at secondary school I was very excited to wear a pair of jeans with rainbow-coloured fringes. I thought they were cool, but the other people in my form probably thought they were a bit weird!

Words of wisdom

Starting secondary school is a really exciting time! Enjoy getting to know as many people as possible, and try out as many different extra-curricular activities as you can. You might find something you didn't know you were good at, you'll make friends much more quickly and it'll help you to feel at home in the school.

Top teacher tips

> Ask as many questions as you can in your first few days/weeks about how the school works. All staff – and most students – will be aware that you're new and will be keen to look out for you.

> Go to your lessons with an open mind – I hated science at primary school but found it a lot more fun at secondary school!

> Get your school bag ready the night before so you don't forget things like pens, pencils, PE kit, and anything else beginning with P!

Dos and Don'ts

> DO make a note of information like room numbers, lesson times and teacher names in your planner. It's often hard to remember details like that in the first few really intense days.

> DO follow the rules which are there to keep you safe, but DON'T worry if you accidentally get something wrong – teachers won't be trying to catch you out.

I ROCK!

A PARENT'S POINT OF VIEW

My name is Alicia and my son is Kezi. He attends Walton High School. When it was time for him to go to high school, we were both a bit upset and fearful, especially since his birthday is in August, which means that he is among the youngest in his year. He's my only child and I was afraid to let him loose in a vast school where there would be hundreds of much older children. The thought of him being bullied or even getting lost in that massive building filled me with trepidation!

However, when we found out that the school was opening for the first two days of the term in September for Year 7s only, we were delighted. That was helpful, as the students would have the opportunity to get to know the place and their teachers. They also began to form new relationships with other students their age – without feeling intimidated by older students. On his first day, I prayed with Kezi before he left, as I do each day, told him I loved him, and then I simply left him in God's care. Although during the day I wondered how he was coping, I was not afraid of anything terrible happening to him. Whenever I thought of him, I would breathe a quick prayer.

Now, further down the line, I am thankful to God that Kezi is settled and getting on as a student very well.

Co-ordinates

negative
positive

y

9
8
7
6
5
4

$A=(2,2)$ $B=(2,-4)$
$c=(-5,-4)$
$d=(-4,1)$

$x + y$
both positive

x $(4,4)$

$(-1,1)x$

HOMEWORK 101

IMPORTANT! Do other things! ...sport, clubs, time with friends. We are not designed to work 24-7... Rest – Relax – Revise – Work

> **Be organised and plan.** Different subjects will require different levels of time – don't leave big projects until the last minute.

> **Mix it up!** Don't just stick to your favourite subjects – you need to do all of them – but use them to keep yourself interested.

> **Use the homework planner** from your new school, or design your own timetable – remember to factor in evenings when you're out doing other things and make up for the time in advance.

> **Bite-size chunks** are better than looooong stretches. Work for 20–30 minutes then stop, have a mini break (5–10 minutes, not a whole TV show!) and then go back.

> **Ask at school for advice** and suggestions on how much time you should be spending on your homework.

> **Ask for help** from teachers and ask for encouragement and support from your parent(s)/guardians. These people are there to help you and have your best interests at heart.

> **Homework IS part of school,** and will get even more important as you go on. So take the time to get into good habits now!

Wayne Dixon is a Schools Development Worker for Scripture Union in the South East region. His top tips...?

Give of your best – Achieve your potential!

It's easy to forget all that homework – write it down!

SURVIVING AT SECONDARY SCHOOL!

- **Make a good first impression.** You have to be there, and if your teachers like you it will make things much easier.

- **Choose your friends wisely.** Don't make friends in a panic and then realise they are the type of friends that get you into trouble.

- **Keep your head up in the corridor** because if there is a crush, it's going to hurt. Think meerkat!

- **If you are late to class** because you got lost, be polite and apologise – your teacher will understand.

- **Hang around in a group** at lunch and break, while you are still settling in. You'll feel safer.

- **Don't pretend to be someone you're not** just to make friends. You are amazing just the way you are!

- **If you see someone being bullied,** tell a teacher you trust that it's going on.

- **If you're worried** about something, why not talk to God about it?

Andrew has been a schools worker in Stockport for seven years and works in both primary and secondary schools. He spends lots of time with Year 6s, chatting to them about their hopes, fears and dreams of secondary school!

Andrew was very shy at school; in fact he was so quiet that some teachers didn't even know his name by the time he was in Year 11! His dad used to go into school to take assemblies – embarrassing! – but now Andrew does exactly the same thing!